MW00356224

# The See and Say Series

You are holding a reproduction of an original work that is in the public domain in the United States of America, and possibly other countries.You may freely copy and distribute this work as no entity (individual or corporate) has a copyright on the body of the work.This book may contain prior copyright references, and library stamps (as most of these works were scanned from library copies).These have been scanned and retained as part of the historical artifact.

This book may have occasional imperfections such as missing or blurred pages, poor pictures, errant marks, etc. that were either part of the original artifact, or were introduced by the scanning process.  We believe this work is culturally important, and despite the imperfections, have elected to bring it back into print as part of our continuing commitment to the preservation of printed works worldwide. We appreciate your understanding of the imperfections in the preservation process, and hope you enjoy this valuable book.

# THE SEE AND SAY SERIES
## BOOK ONE

❀

### A PICTURE BOOK TEACHING
### THE LETTERS AND THEIR
### SOUNDS WITH LESSONS IN
### WORD BUILDING

BY

SARAH LOUISE ARNOLD
ELIZABETH C. BONNEY AND
E. F. SOUTHWORTH

## GINN · AND · COMPANY
### BOSTON · NEW YORK · CHICAGO · LONDON

COPYRIGHT, 1913, BY SARAH LOUISE ARNOLD, ELIZABETH C. BONNEY
AND E. F. SOUTHWORTH
ALL RIGHTS RESERVED
413.5

Harvard University
Dept. of Education Library
Gift of the Publishers

JUL − 2 1913

TRANSFERRED TO
HARVARD COLLEGE LIBRARY

1930

The Athenæum Press
GINN AND COMPANY · PRO-
PRIETORS · BOSTON · U.S.A.

2

## To Those who place this Book in
## the hands of Children
## Greeting :

The See and Say books are intended to enable children to master the form and sound of words.

This word mastery is an indispensable factor of reading; it is also essential to spelling. If the child can obtain a clue to the pronunciation of new words, he becomes independent of the teacher and can help himself in reading; further, his knowledge of the sounds of the letters furnishes a key to spelling all words which are spelled in accordance with phonic laws.

In former days children were taught to read by the slow and inadequate process of learning the alphabet, pronouncing the letters of every new word and waiting to hear the word pronounced by the teacher. Sometimes this spelling furnished the young learner with a clue to the pronunciation of the word, and sometimes not.

The word and sentence methods attempted to correct the errors of the alphabet method. These methods emphasized the truth that words are merely signs of ideas and that sentences exist to express thought. By these methods, we said, reading should become what it ought to be — getting the thought from the printed page. Every new word so learned by itself was the sign of an idea; in the sentence it helped to express the thought. Children thus taught learned to read with expression, but were wholly dependent upon the teacher when confronted by an unfamiliar word. When later they were asked to spell and write, their reading had provided little aid.

3

## 4

The phonic method of teaching reading then attempted to correct the word and sentence methods. Elaborate systems were introduced to teach reading as based upon the sounds of words; series of reading books were created, whose lessons were composed of words having given sounds. This naturally proved impossible as a method of teaching reading, for the form of the word became so important as to exclude all reference to the idea, and the reading lesson had little intrinsic interest for the children.

The See and Say books propose to separate the study of words from the lesson in reading. By the aid of these books children should pronounce independently the words composing the ordinary vocabulary, so that they may readily read for themselves the various school readers presenting such a selected vocabulary. After learning that every letter represents a specific sound, as in the case of most consonants, or several sounds, as in the case of certain vowels, they ought by this means to master the large majority of words presented in their reading books.

They should be so trained, therefore, that the letter, or combination of letters, will *at once* suggest the sound. The printed word, then, would stand for the *spoken word with its idea.* When the idea is new the teacher of reading will present it; but if the form of the word only is new, the child should be able to pronounce the word for himself.

Of course there are difficulties in the way. In the English language certain letters stand for different sounds, and the same sound is often represented by different letters or groups of letters; but even with this difficulty the mastery of large groups of similar words is easily possible.

The See and Say books present a simple method of word mastery. The first book is like the picture book which has always been fascinating to the child. He has turned its pages at home, has named the various objects in the pictures, has mooed like the cow, or growled like the dog, or said " choo, choo," when he

saw the engine or cars. Book One therefore presents a picture
to suggest the sound of each letter. It also pictures an object
whose initial sound is the sound of the letter. M stands for the
sound which the cow makes when calling her calf, which is
also the first sound of "moon." The child, dealing with the pictures just as he has done at home, associates the sound M with
the story, with the picture, with the word "moon," and with
the letter. With repetition the *association of sound and letter* is
just as prompt and effective as the association of picture and
name, or picture and sound.

This book, then, takes advantage of what the child already
knows and what he loves to do. It builds on this foundation
simple and adequate knowledge of the sounds of each letter of
the alphabet. The short sounds of the vowels have been selected
for these are more used than any others. It has been necessary
to add the fact that *s* has two sounds, and that the sound of *k*
is also represented by *c* and *ck*. A few vowels, as well as consonants, are presented in combination, as, *oi, oy, ou, ow, oo, ee,
sh, ch, th.*

It is a short step from the picture book of the nursery to Book
One of the See and Say Series. This is a simple and natural
step and is extremely important. *Here the study of the book is
presented in its simplest form.* If the child forgets the sound of *a*,
he turns to the picture of the baby reaching for the apple, and
the picture reminds him of the sound. He can do this independently and thus learns to use the book and understand its use.
This is one of the great advantages attaching to this method of
presenting words. Not only is the overburdened teacher assisted
by the book in the hands of the children, but with this book as
a tool the child becomes at once independent of the teacher.

The Series consists of four books intended for the children,
each book being accompanied by a teacher's manual which out-
lines the work to be done by the teacher. These manuals suggest

a large variety of exercises which afford the necessary practice without the dullness of ordinary repetition. Book One is a picture book, teaching the letters of the alphabet with their ordinary sounds. Book Two and Book Three are Word Books, giving attention to further sounds of the letters and teaching all phonograms or syllables which are frequently repeated in the ordinary vocabulary. Book Four reviews the material of the earlier books and presents in an orderly series the fundamental laws of phonics as applied to spelling. In addition, the words which must be taught by sight, since they vary from phonetic spelling, are introduced and taught. By means of the series word mastery is assured.

The authors are confident that the See and Say Series will relieve reading of its burdens and lessen the time given heretofore to the teaching of reading; will give the child a clear knowledge of the form and sound of English words; will teach him the use of the book as a tool; will remove obstacles in the way of spelling; and will greatly relieve the overworked teacher in our crowded schools.

Miss Sarah C. Brooks, formerly Director of the Training School for Teachers, Baltimore, and previously Supervisor of Primary Schools in St. Paul, has given generous assistance in the arrangement of the lessons and in criticism of the plan. For this aid the authors wish to express their grateful appreciation.

# KEY SENTENCES

## WHICH ARE TO BE LEARNED IN CONNECTION WITH THE PICTURES PRESENTING THE SOUNDS OF THE LETTERS

A   When baby wants an apple he says *a*, and *a* is the first sound of "apple." Page 12.

B   Water bubbling out of a bottle says *b*, and *b* is the first sound of " ball." Page 34.

C   When the pop corn sticks in the boy's throat he says *c*, and *c* is the first sound of " cat." (The sound of *c*, hard, is first taught with *k*.) Page 71.

D   The doves say *d*, and *d* is the first sound of "doll." Page 67.

E   The big round saw says *e*, and *e* is the first sound of "egg." Page 41.

F   The cross cat says *f*, and *f* is the first sound of " flag." Page 42.

G   The frog says *g*, and *g* is the first sound of "girl." Page 81.

H   The tired dog says *h*, and *h* is the first sound of "hat." Page 84.

I   The little pig says *i*, and *i* is the first sound of " ink." Page 62.

J   The motor boat says *j*, and *j* is the first sound of "jam." Page 79.

K   When the pop corn sticks in the boy's throat he says *k*, and *k* is the first sound of " kite." Page 71.

L   The telegraph wires say *l*, and *l* is the first sound of "lily." Page 15.

M   The cow says *m*, and *m* is the first sound of "moon." Page 9.

N   The calf says *n*, and *n* is the first sound of "nest." Page 24.

O   When baby sees the hot lamp she says *o*, and *o* is the first sound of "orange." Page 30.

P   The tugboat says *p*, and *p* is the first sound of "pig." Page 39.

Qu   When the ducks begin to talk they say *qu, qu* (whisper it), and *qu* is the first sound of "queen." Page 97.

R   The dog says *r*, and *r* is the first sound of "rat." Page 21.

S   The snake says *s*, and *s* is the first sound of "swan." Page 18.

T   The watch says *t*, and *t* is the first sound of "top." Page 59.

U    When baby wants to be taken up she says *u*, and *u* is the first sound of "umbrella." Page 86.

V    The electric car says *v*, and *v* is the first sound of "vase." Page 90.

W    The wind says *w*, and *w* is the first sound of "wing." Page 94.

X    While the engine waits for you to get on the train it says *ks(x)*, and *x* is the last sound of "fox." Page 101.

Y    When the scissors are being sharpened they say *y*, and *y* is the first sound of "yard." Page 100.

Z    The bee says *z*, and *z* is the first sound of "zebra." Page 27.

CH    The engine when it goes says *ch*, and *ch* is the first sound of "church." Page 49.

SH    Mother says *sh* when baby is asleep, and *sh* is the first sound of "shell." Page 51.

CK    Has the sound of *k*; it is the last sound of "clock." Page 71.

EE    The little mice in the trap say *ee*, and *ee* is the first sound of "eel." Page 96.

NG    The bell says *ng*, and *ng* is the last sound of "gong." Page 103.

OO    When we feel cold we say *oo*, and *oo* is in the word "spoon." Page 107.

OY    The oyster man says *oy*, and *oy* is the first sound of "oyster." Page 110.

OI    Has the same sound as *oy*. Page 110.

OW    When hurt we say *ow*, and *ow* is the first sound of "owl." Page 114.

OU    Sometimes has the same sound as *ow*. Page 114.

TH    The goose says *th*, and *th* is the first sound of "thimble." Page 117.

m                                    M

m            m            m

m   M      moon

m                moon                M

M          m          m          M

Moon        moon

a A

a a a

A a

apple

a apple A

a  A

apple

A

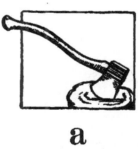

a

|  | A |  |
|---|---|---|
| a | a | m |
| apple | m | moon |
| Apple | M | Moon |

m       M

M m       A a       M m

moon

apple

A a

A a

l  L

l  l  l

L  l

lily

lily  lily  Lily

l

L

l

l

l

L

L

l

Lily

m      a      l

M      A      L

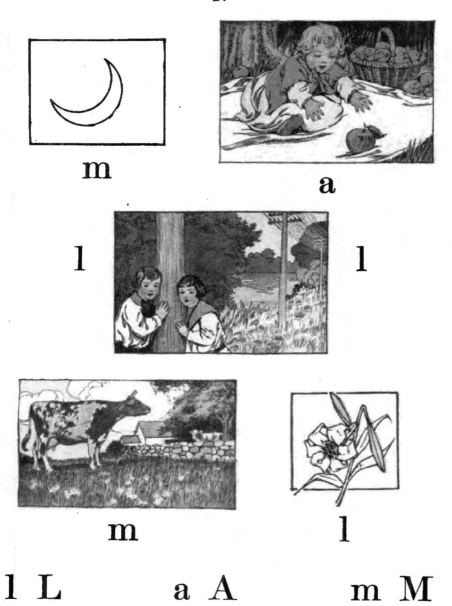

m

a

l

l

m

l

l L      a A      m M

s                                    S

s              s              s

S                                    s

swan

swan

s              swan              S

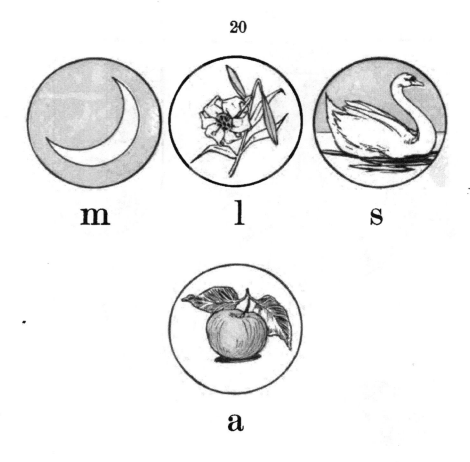

m  l  s

a

moon      lily      am
apple      swan      Sam

M m      A a      L l      S s

r · R

r · r · r

r · R

rat

R · rat · r

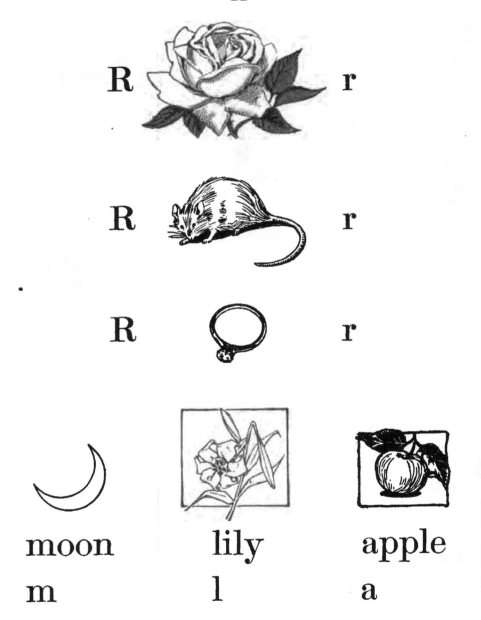

R      r

R      r

R      r

moon     lily     apple

m       l       a

rat

rats

apple

apples

swan

swans

| rat | apple | swan |
|------|--------|-------|
| rats | apples | swans |

n                  N

n        n        n

N               n

nest

n          nest         N

m         moon      M

n  N

n N

n N

m   moon          swan   s

| a A | r R | n N |
|-----|-----|-----|
| m moon | M Moon | |
| a apple | A Apple | |
| l lily | L Lily | |
| r rat | R Rat | |
| s swan | S Swan | |
| n nest | N Nest | |
| m M | l L | s S |

z                                    Z

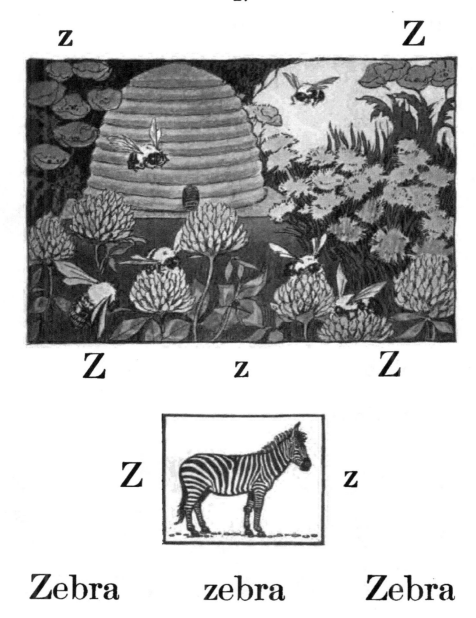

Z               z               Z

Z                               z

Zebra          zebra          Zebra

| r | rat | R |
|---|---|---|
| l | lily | L |
| a | apple | A |
| m | moon | M |
| s | swan | S |

| moon | moons |
|---|---|
| apple | apples |
| rat | rats |
| swan | swans |

| m | moon |
|---|------|
| a | apple |
| l | lily |
| n | nest |
| r | rat |
| s | swan |
| z | zebra |

Swans    Nests

Apples    Rats

o                                 O

o           o           o

O                  o

## orange

O         orange         o

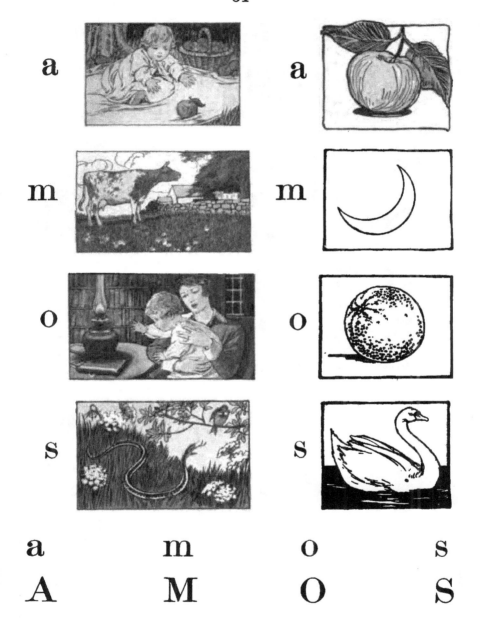

a a

m m

o o

s s

a     m     o     s

A     M     O     S

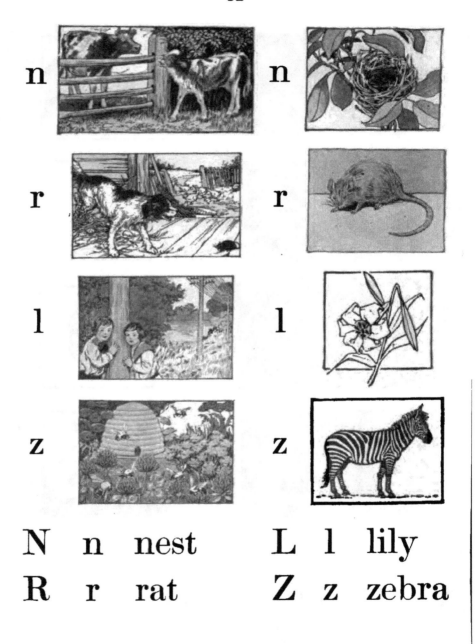

N n nest     L l lily

R r rat     Z z zebra

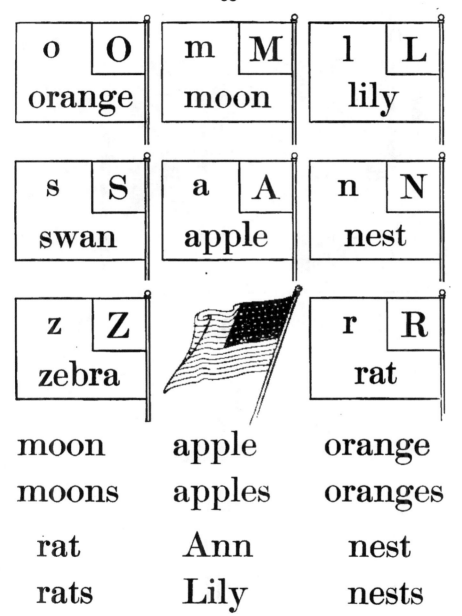

| o O | m M | l L |
| orange | moon | lily |
| s S | a A | n N |
| swan | apple | nest |
| z Z | | r R |
| zebra | | rat |

| moon | apple | orange |
| moons | apples | oranges |
| rat | Ann | nest |
| rats | Lily | nests |

b          B

b          b          b

B          b

ball

b          ball          B

b
B

a    m

n    l

b
B

b    B

o    r

s    z

b

B    b

b
B

A    M

N    L

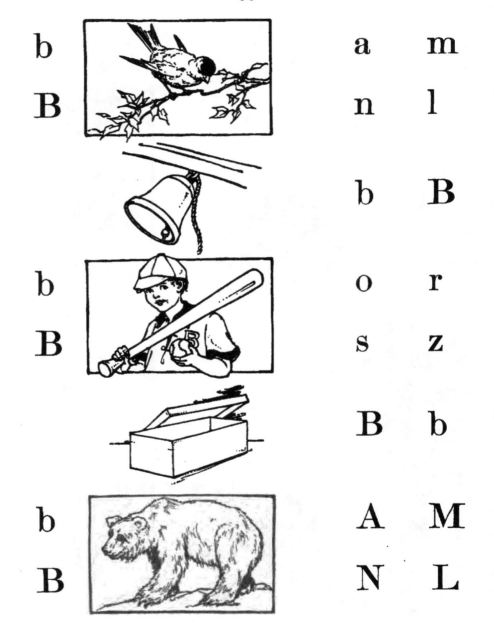

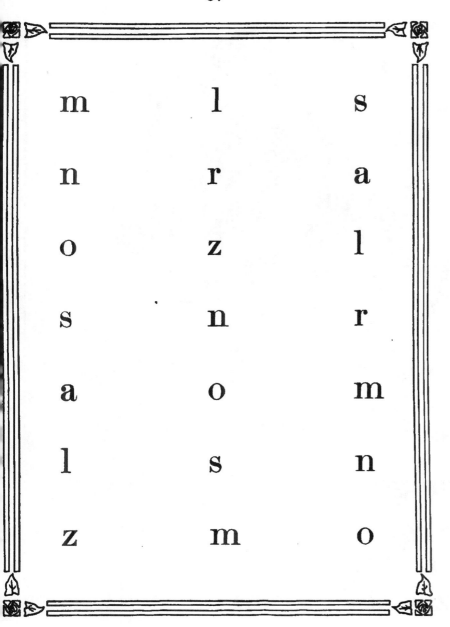

| m | l | s |
| n | r | a |
| o | z | l |
| s | n | r |
| a | o | m |
| l | s | n |
| z | m | o |

| Apple | Moon | Nest |
|-------|------|------|
| apple | moon | nest |
| Orange | Rat | Swan |
| orange | rat | swan |
| zebra | Ball | Lily |

p
P

p p p

p p

pig

| p | pig | b | ball | r | rat |
|---|-----|---|------|---|-----|
| P | Pigs | B | Balls | R | Rats |

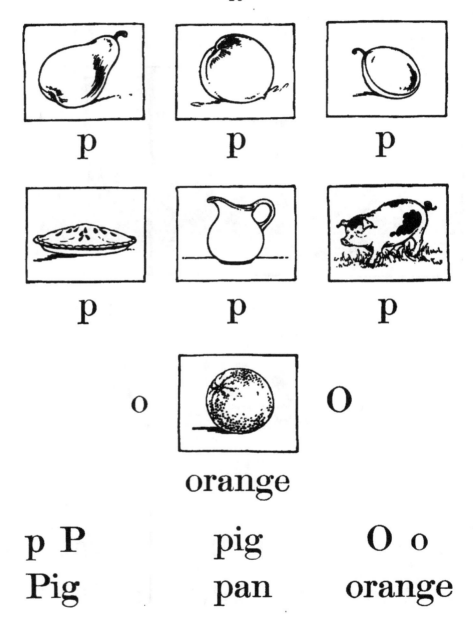

p     p     p

p     p     p

o     O

orange

p P     pig     O o
Pig     pan     orange

e
E

e
e
e

E
e

Egg 
egg

egg

p      e      o      b      m

P      E      O      B      M

f    f    f

F    f

flag

F f        flag        f F

fan

f F Flags F f

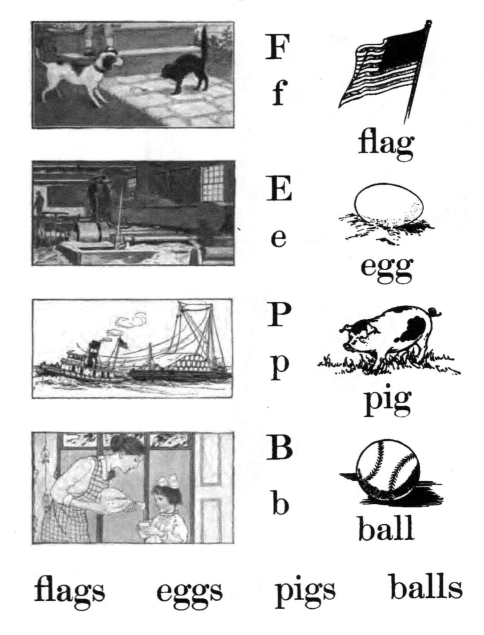

F f

flag

E e

egg

P p

pig

B b

ball

flags    eggs    pigs    balls

| apple | nest | moon |
| a | n | m |
| am | Nan | map |
| | | |
| swan | ball | rat |
| s | b | r |
| sop | Ben | rap |
| | | |
| lily | flag | pig |
| l | f | p |
| lap | fan | pan |
| | | |
| egg | orange | pens |
| e | on | fans |

KATHARINE R WIREMAN

p   a   n

p  a n

pan

f   a   n

f  a n

fan

B   e   n

B  e n

Ben

| fan | pen | lap |
|-----|-----|-----|
| pan | fen | nap |
| man | men | map |

ch                                    Ch

ch    ch    ch

Ch                        ch

ch          church              op
Ch          Church              chop

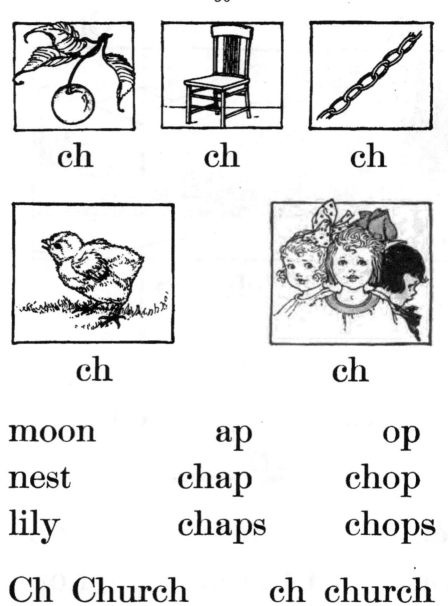

ch          ch          ch

ch                    ch

moon            ap              op
nest           chap            chop
lily           chaps           chops

Ch Church      ch church

sh          Sh

sh          sh          sh

Sh                    sh

shell

sh      she ll      shell      Sh

sh  ch  p  f  b  e  o  z  n  r  s

# Sh

sh                              sh

sh              sh

sh              sh

shell                            shop
shells       shops

| m M | a A | l L |
|-----|-----|-----|
| s S | r R | n N |
| o O | b B | p P |
| e E | f F | z Z |

| sh Sh | ch Ch | sh Sh |
|-------|-------|-------|

| moon | apple | lily |
|------|-------|------|
| swan | rat | nest |
| orange | ball | pig |
| egg | flag | shell |
| church | | zebra |

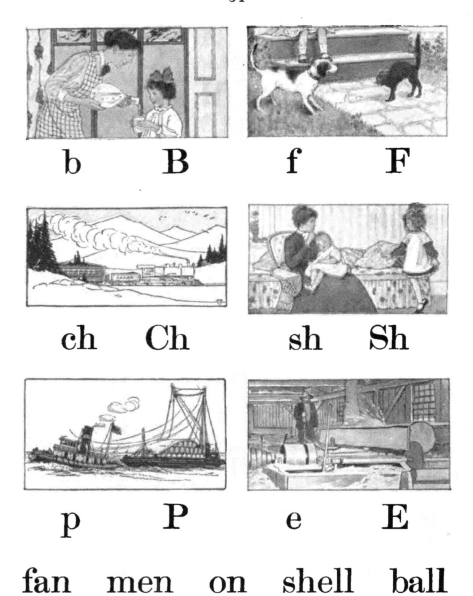

b　　B　　　f　　F

ch　Ch　　　sh　Sh

p　　P　　　e　　E

fan　men　on　shell　ball

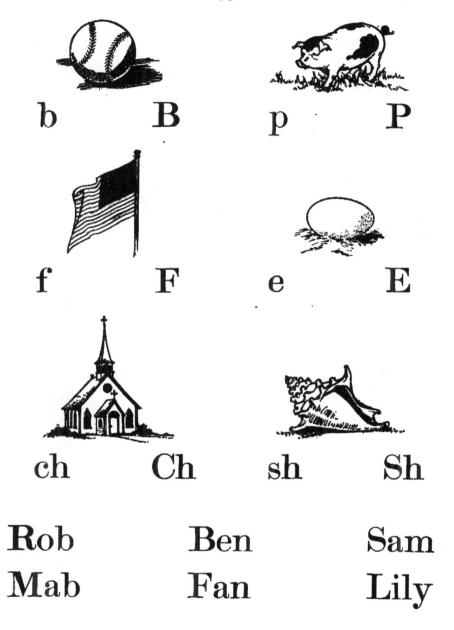

b    B        p    P

f    F        e    E

ch    Ch    sh    Sh

Rob    Ben    Sam

Mab    Fan    Lily

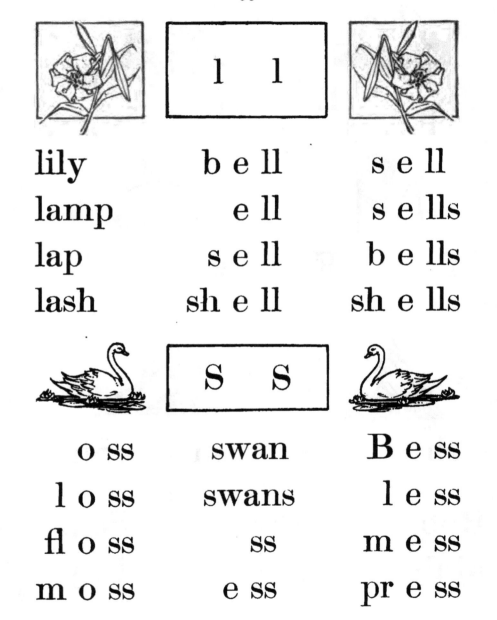

| l | l |

lily        b e ll        s e ll

lamp       e ll        s e lls

lap        s e ll       b e lls

lash      sh e ll     sh e lls

| S | S |

o ss       swan      B e ss

l o ss     swans     l e ss

fl o ss      ss      m e ss

m o ss     e ss      pr e ss

e

egg

b

ball

ch

church

p

pig

sh

shell

|        |       |       |        |
|--------|-------|-------|--------|
| shell  | pen   | mop   | lap    |
| bell   | men   | chop  | chap   |
| fell   | fen   | chops | rap    |
| sell   | Ben   | shops | map    |

| egg  | apple  | orange  |
|------|--------|---------|
| eggs | apples | oranges |

t                                    T

t                                    t

T          t

top

| top  | T   | tap |
|------|-----|-----|
| tops | Tom | ten |

t r a p

trap

m a p

map

T  t

r a t

rat

b a t

bat

T
t

t e n t

tent

s e n t

sent

| N a t | N a n |
|-------|-------|
| **N** a t | **N** a n |
| r a t | m a n |
| r a t | m a n |
| b a t | f a n |
| b a t | f a n |
| p a t | t a n |
| p a t | t a n |
| f a t | r a n |
| f a t | r a n |
| m a t | p a n |
| mats | pans |

i         I

i     i     i

I          i

ink

| pin | sit | tent | ship |
|-----|-----|------|------|
| in  | it  | ent  | ip   |
| spin | lit | sent | lip |

| ink | ship | fish |
| Ink | Ship | Fish |

| t ip | ch ip | n ip |
| r ip | l ip | s ip |

| in | | ill |
| fin | | pill |
| bin | fist | spill |
| pin | list | till |
| pins | fists | mills |

n

n e s t       at

nest       rat

r

r a t       mat

rat       pat

sh

sh o p       not

shop       spot

sh

sh e ll       bell

shell       spell

shells       spells

| rat | flag | rob |
|------|-------|------|
| rats | flags | robs |
| shell | man | egg |
| shells | men | eggs |
| pig | bell | shop |
| pigs | bells | shops |
| Tom | sat | bell |
| not | ran | man |
| spot | fell | am |

| at | at | at | at |
|-----|-----|-----|-----|
| bat | rat | Nat | sat |

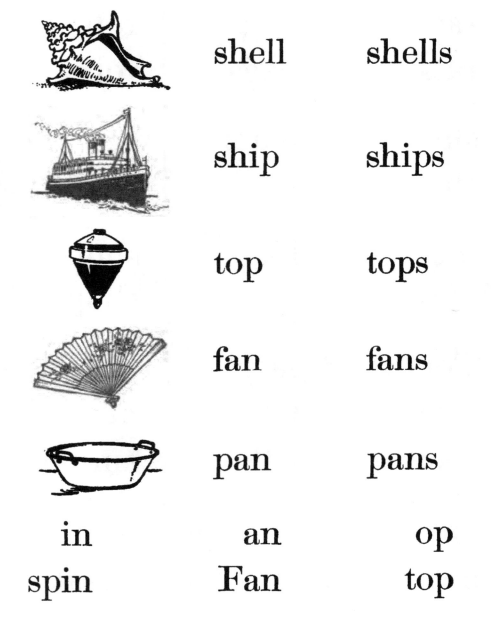

shell     shells

ship     ships

top     tops

fan     fans

pan     pans

in     an     op

spin     Fan     top

d          D

`d      d      d

D      d

doll

| doll | Ned | did |
|------|-----|-----|
| Dan | sled | den |

d   i   t   sh   ch   f   e   m   a   l

d     D     d     D

d

d

d

d

N e d

s l e d

d i sh

d o ll

D o n

D a n

Ned   top

fed  red  Ned

r e d t o p

s p i n

Spin, red top, spin.

a n d  s t a n d  top

and   stand  spin

## Dan and Bess

zebra    rat    doll    swan    pig

Z z    R r    D d    S s    P p

doll    din    did    dish    dip

ch    sh    e    f    o    b    l    n

Ch    Sh    E    F    O    B    L    N

C       ck       K

c       ck       k

cat       clock       kite

c       ck       k

C       ck       K

c C    k K    ck

lock    cat    cap    kit

clocks    cats    caps    milk

b B    p P    e E    f F

| ball | pig | egg | flag |
|------|-----|-----|------|
| Ball | Pig | Egg | Flag |
| balls | pigs | eggs | flags |

| fan | moon | men | map |
|-----|------|-----|-----|
| Fan | Moon | Men | Map |
| fans | moons | pens | maps |

| nap | rap | dash | fed |
|-----|-----|------|-----|
| Nap | Rap | Dash | Bed |
| naps | raps | lash | red |

A
a
apple

D
d
doll

E
e
egg

F
f
flag

I
i
ink

b      B

B     b

**Ball**     ball

cat 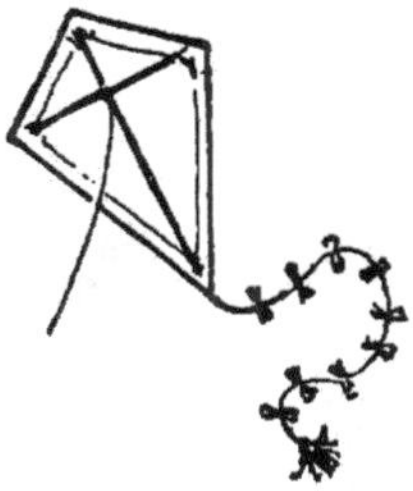     kite      clock

c C    ck    k K

L l    lily

M m    moon

N n    nest

O o    orange

P p    pig

R r    rat

S s    swan

T t    top

Z z    zebra

Ch ch    church

| Ned | Dick  | sit  |
| fed | kick  | let  |
| led | rick  | trot |
| bed | stick | back |

j              J

j      j      j

jet     J        j     jot
jib                   jŏb

jam

Jack     jam     Jill

M L R Z B E Ch T K

# J                            j

| Jack | a m | Jill |
|------|-----|------|
| can | j a m | rill |
| fell | S a m | spill |
| tell | sh a m | doll |

| am | | ill |
|----|----|-----|
| jam | | fill |

| J | Dick | j |
|------|------|-----|
| Jack | sick | job |

g                   G

g       g       g

G            g

**girl**

| G | got | get | gap | glad |
|---|-----|-----|-----|------|
| g | frog | dog | log | gas |

G

g    G

g    G

g    G

g

| nag | egg | eggs | beg |
|-----|------|-------|-----|
| rag | dog | dogs | leg |
| tag | log | logs | peg |
| bag | frog | frogs | big |

frog    dog    log

big   dig     frog   log

pig   fig     dog   fog

egg   eggs     frog   frogs

leg    beg    peg

legs   begs   pegs

h        H

h     h     h

H       h

hat

Has    hat    Hand

g j k ck d i t sh c f p

hod                ham

hog                              hem

hop                              him

hot                              hill

h

hat                hats

hand                         hands

hat

| hop | him | hot |
|-----|-----|-----|
| hops | his | lot |
| hen | had | not |
| hens | has | spot |

u                                    U

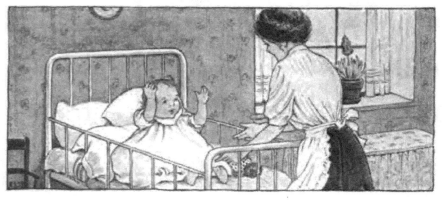

u            u            u

U  u

umbrella

| up  | sun | u   U      |
|-----|-----|-----------|
| cup | gun | drum      |
| pup | fun | umbrella  |

u       U

| | | |
|---|---|---|
| up | | ut |
| cup | | cut |
| pup | | nut |

| um | un | ust |
|---|---|---|
| hum | bun | dust |
| drum | fun | rust |
| chum | gun | crust |

| | | |
|---|---|---|
| | ump | u |
| | bump | U |
| umbrella | lump | u |

jump          up

pump           cup

lump           cups

umbrella

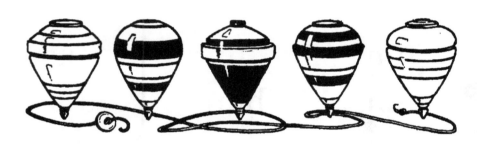

Tops spin and hum.

top         stop         hop

tops        stops       hops

hat              hut

hats                   huts

i I

t T

d D

G
g

j J

V  V

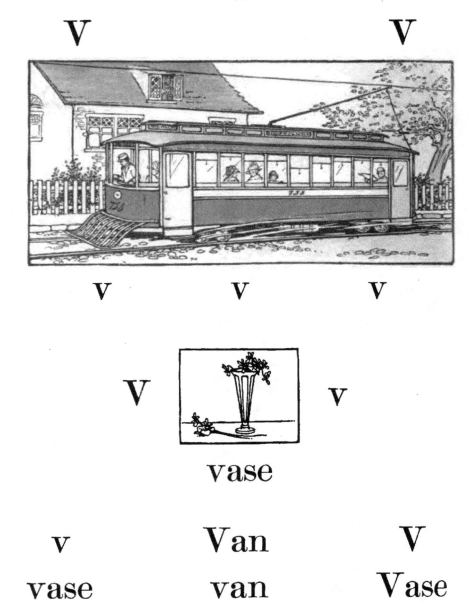

V  V  V

V  v

vase

v  Van  V

vase  van  Vase

| Ann | Tom | Fred | Jill |
|------|-------|------|------|
| Bess | Dick | Don | Nell |
| Fan | Jack | Ned | Nat |
| Lily | Meg | Ben | Rob |
| Nan | Frank | Dan | Bell |

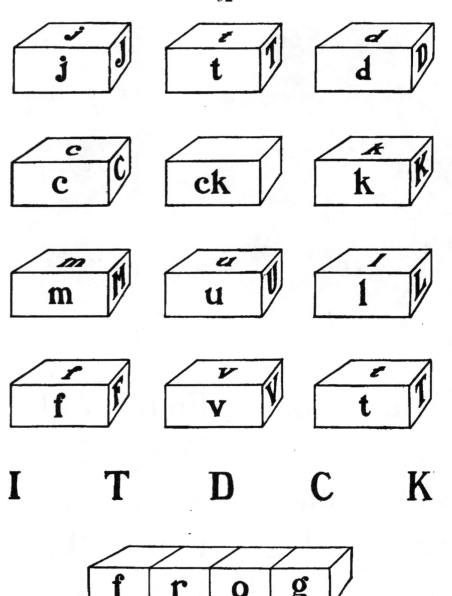

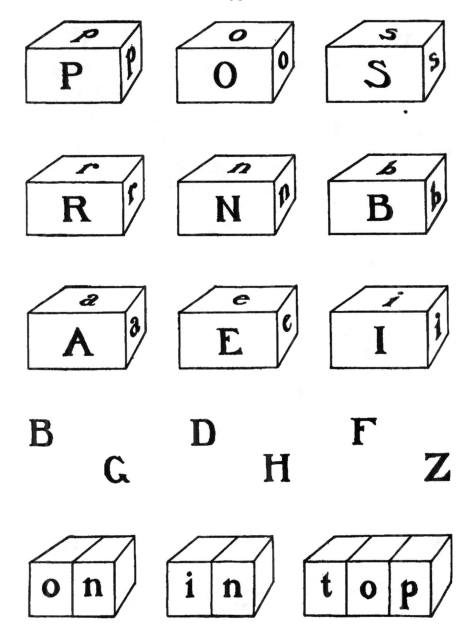

w　　　　　　　　　　W

w　　　　w　　　　w

W　　　　　　　　w

wing

well　　　　w　　　　will
wet　　　　W　　　　wind

h　u　v　w　g　j　l　c　b　p

wet  wit

web wilt

w       w

w       w

w i n       w ing       w e st

w i ll       w ind       w e ll

w i ck       w ish       w e nt

van       vest       vel vet

pin    spin    span    spun

pins    spins    pans    puns

ee                Ee

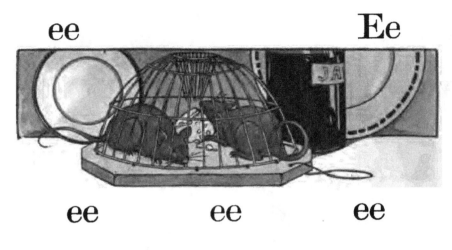

ee         ee         ee

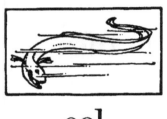

eel

| ee | eel | meet | sheep |
|------|-------|--------|-------|
| see | feel | beet | creep |
| bee | feels | feet | sleep |
| sees | peel | street | deep |

qu        Qu

qu       qu       qu

Qu        qu

queen

qu ee n      qu ee r
qu i ck      qu a ck

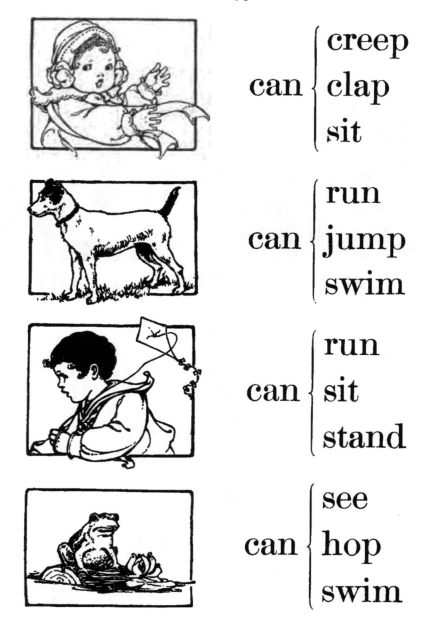

can { creep
clap
sit

can { run
jump
swim

can { run
sit
stand

can { see
hop
swim

# Skip! Hop! Jump!

Skip and hop and jump!

| a | e | i | o | u |
|---|---|---|---|---|
| cat | neck | hill | on | cup |
| bag | bed | tip | off | mud |
| sat | lend | mist | hot | cud |
| cab | best | rich | not | fun |

y          Y

y       y       y

y
Y         yard

y       yet       yam

Y       yes       yell

qu     ee     ch     ck     sh

x X

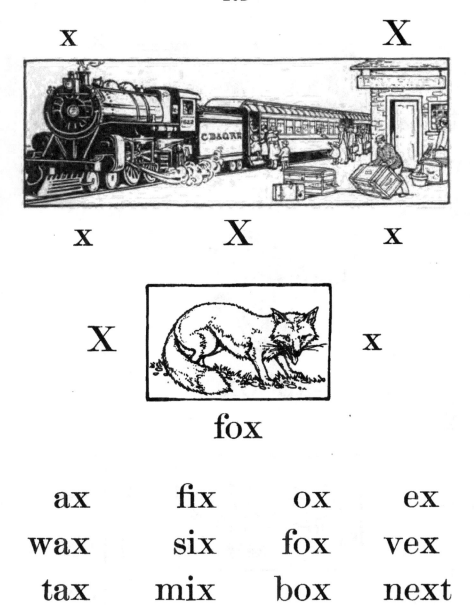

x X x

X x

fox

| ax | fix | ox | ex |
| wax | six | fox | vex |
| tax | mix | box | next |

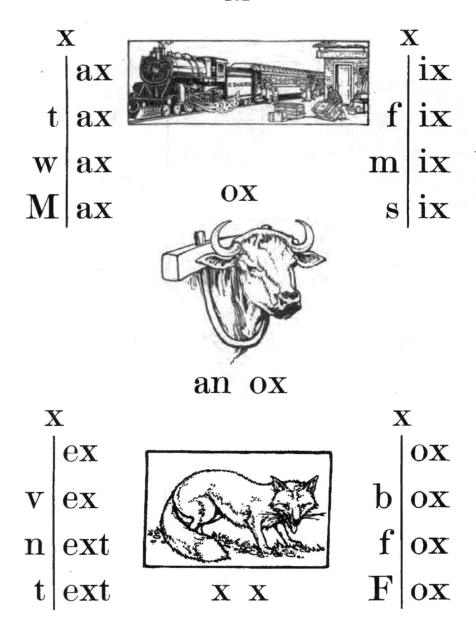

x | ax
t | ax
w | ax
M | ax

x | ix
f | ix
m | ix
s | ix

ox

an ox

x | ex
v | ex
n | ext
t | ext

x x

x | ox
b | ox
f | ox
F | ox

ng                      ng

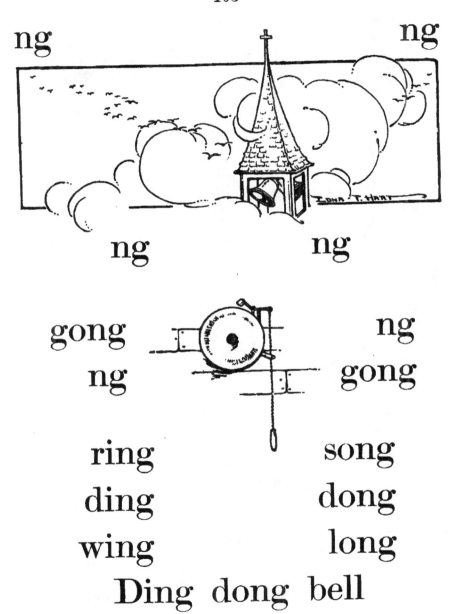

ng            ng

gong                ng

ng                  gong

ring           song

ding          dong

wing         long

Ding dong bell

X x    **fox**

Y y    **yard**

U u    **umbrella**

V v    **vase**

ng ng    **gong**

| a | e | i | u |
|---|---|---|---|
| o | b | f | v |
| c | ck | k | ee |
| d | ch | g | x |
| j | l | m | n |
| qu | p | r | ng |
| s | t | sh | y |
| z | w | h | ss |

| a | e | i | o | u |
|---|---|---|---|---|

| d | o | g | | h | a | s |
|---|---|---|---|---|---|---|
| l | o | ck | | b | a | t |
| r | o | t | | c | a | n |

| m | e | t | | h | u | m |
|---|---|---|---|---|---|---|
| p | e | n | | r | u | n |
| f | e | d | | f | u | n |

| r | u | sh | | r | i | ng |
|---|---|---|---|---|---|---|
| r | u | ng | | s | u | ng |

oo                    oo

o͞o                    o͞o

oo          oo

spo͞on

spoon          cool
moon           tool
boot          spool
boots         spools

o͞o

o͝o

o͞o

o͝o

spo͞on     bo͝ok

moon     cook

cool     look

spool     brook

room   broom   good   wood

| r | a | n |
|---|---|---|
| c | a | p |
| r | a | g |

oy oy

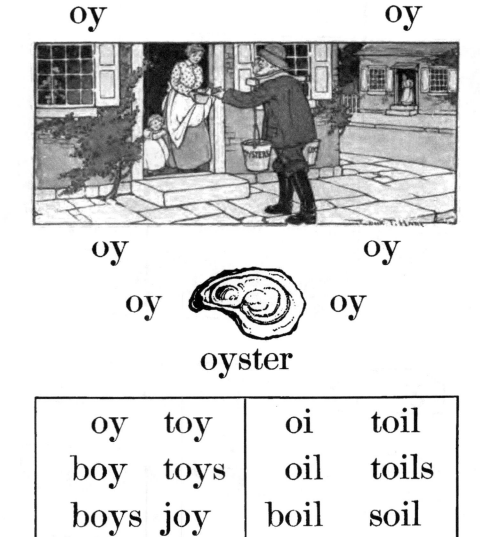

oy oy

oy oy

oyster

| oy | toy | oi | toil |
|------|------|------|-------|
| boy | toys | oil | toils |
| boys | joy | boil | soil |
| Troy | joys | boils | soils |

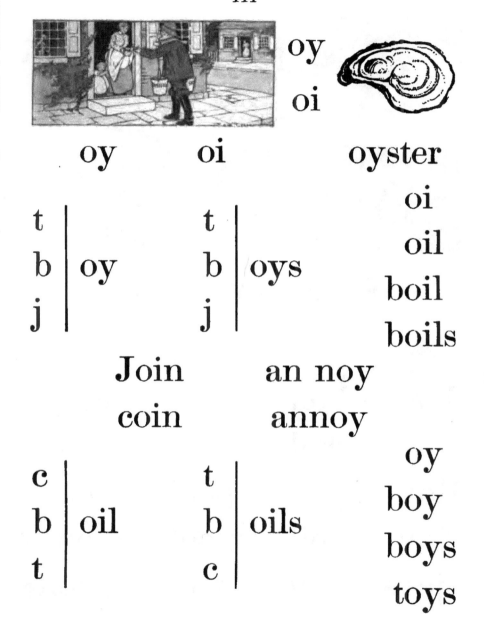

oy

oi

oy      oi      oyster

oi

oil

t

b   oy     t

j         b   oys    boil

j           boils

Join     an noy

coin     annoy

oy

c         t         boy

b   oil    b   oils   boys

t         c        toys

spo͞on

oyster

o͞o     oy     oi

| oy | oil | ool | oon |
|---|---|---|---|
| boy | boil | cool | coon |
| toy | coil | fool | noon |
| Roy | spoil | pool | soon |
| joy | soil | spool | moon |
| joys | toil | tool | spoon |

ow ow

ow ow

ow owl

| ow | owl | ou | loud |
|------|------|------|-------|
| cow | fowl | out | cloud |
| now | howl | pout | shout |

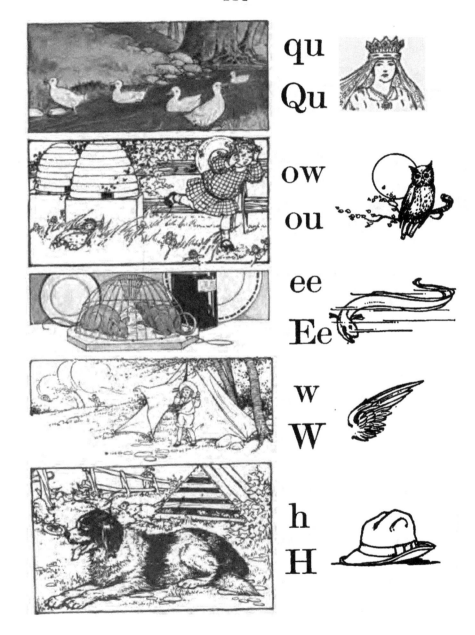

qu
Qu

ow
ou

ee
Ee

w
W

h
H

(ll)　(ss)　(ee)　(o͞o)　(o͝o)

[b]　[f]　[g]　[i]　[d]

✶i✶　✶p✶　✶n✶　✶m✶　✶v✶

[w]　[x]　[y]　[h]　[r]

(oi oy)　(ou ow)　[c k ck]　(ng)　(qu)

qu
Qu

queen     quack     quick

ll          ll

bell    shell      fill    doll

ow
ou      ss

owl     out      oss     iss
fowl   shout     toss    miss

Th                                    th

th          th          th

Th          th

thimble

th          tooth          thin
Th          teeth          thick

| | | | |
|---|---|---|---|
| Th | | th | |
| Th i s | | Th a t | |
| th i s | | th a t | |
| this | | that | |

| | | | |
|---|---|---|---|
| th e m | | th e n | |
| th e m | | th e n | |
| them | | then | |

| | | | |
|---|---|---|---|
| w i th | | this | |
| w i th | | that | |
| with | | them | |

| | | |
|---|---|---|
| thin | thick | thimble |
| them | then | with |

|    |      |       |    |     |
|----|------|-------|----|-----|
| th | in   | th    | th | is  |
|    | ick  | tooth |    | at  |
|    | ank  | teeth |    | em  |
|    | ink  | with  |    | en  |

| oy     | oi    | qu    |
|--------|-------|-------|
| boy    | oil   | queer |
| boys   | boil  | queen |
| toy    | toil  | quill |
| toys   | coin  | quack |
| joys   | join  | quick |
| oyster | joint | quiz  |

miss   bell   loss   dull   kiss

lily

pig

top

cup

doll

eel

mat

rat

dog

frog

ball

sled

shell

spoon

vase

wing

clock

cat

fan

nut

zebra

orange

umbrella

apple

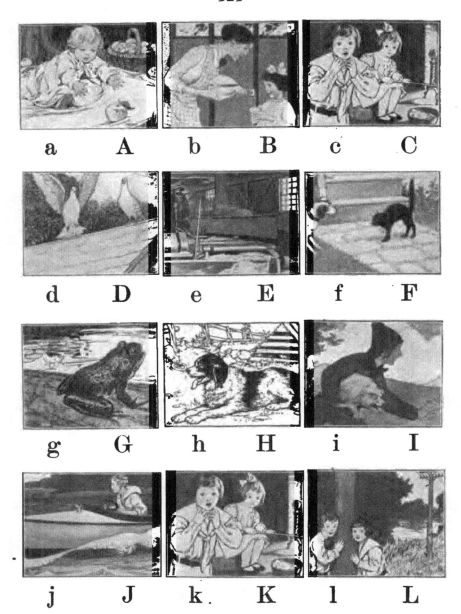

a    A    b    B    c    C

d    D    e    E    f    F

g    G    h    H    i    I

j    J    k.    K    l    L

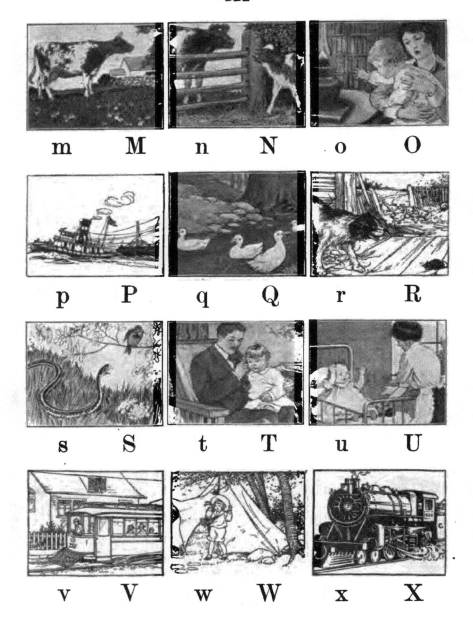

m  M   n  N   o  O

p  P   q  Q   r  R

s  S   t  T   u  U

v  V   w  W   x  X

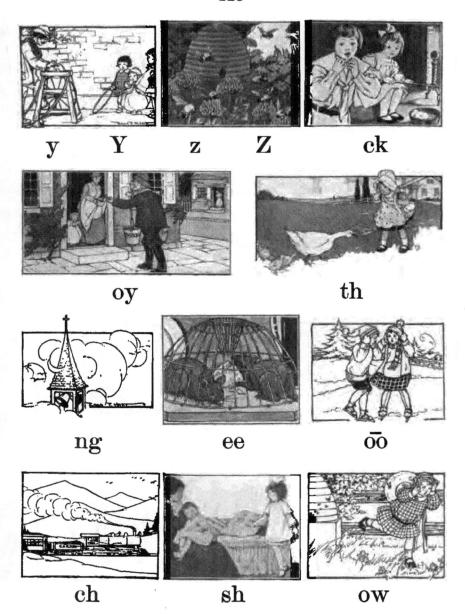

y Y z Z ck

oy th

ng ee ōō

ch sh ow

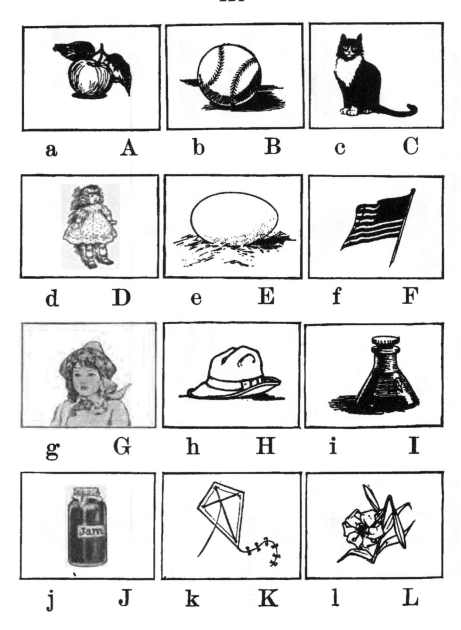

a   A     b   B     c   C

d   D     e   E     f   F

g   G     h   H     i   I

j   J     k   K     l   L

| | | |
|---|---|---|
| m M | n N | o O |
| p P | q Q | r R |
| s S | t T | u U |
| v V | w W | x X |

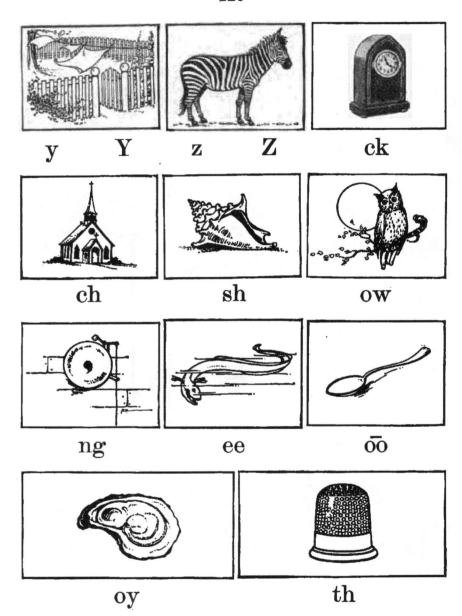

y  Y    z  Z    ck

ch        sh        ow

ng        ee        ōo

oy        th

| | | | |
|---|---|---|---|
| apple<br>A a | ball<br>B b | cat<br>C c | doll<br>D d |
| egg<br>E e | flag<br>F f | girl<br>G g | hat<br>H h |
| ink<br>I i | jam<br>J j | kite<br>K k | lily<br>L l |
| moon<br>M m | nest<br>N n | orange<br>O o | pig<br>P p |
| queen<br>Q q | rat<br>R r | swan<br>S s | top<br>T t |
| umbrella<br>U u | vase<br>V v | wing<br>W w | fox<br>X x |
| yard<br>Y y | | | zebra<br>Z z |

| | | | | |
|---|---|---|---|---|
| a<br><sub>12</sub> | b<br><sub>34</sub> | c<br><sub>71</sub> | d<br><sub>67</sub> | e<br><sub>41</sub> |
| f<br><sub>42</sub> | g<br><sub>81</sub> | h<br><sub>84</sub> | i<br><sub>62</sub> | j<br><sub>79</sub> |
| k<br><sub>71</sub> | l<br><sub>15</sub> | m<br><sub>9</sub> | n<br><sub>24</sub> | o<br><sub>30</sub> |
| p<br><sub>39</sub> | q<br><sub>97</sub> | r<br><sub>21</sub> | s<br><sub>18</sub> | t<br><sub>59</sub> |
| u<br><sub>86</sub> | v<br><sub>90</sub> | w<br><sub>94</sub> | x<br><sub>101</sub> | y<br><sub>100</sub> |
| z<br><sub>27</sub> | ck<br><sub>71</sub> | ch<br><sub>49</sub> | sh<br><sub>51</sub> | ng<br><sub>103</sub> |
| oo<br><sub>107</sub> | ow<br><sub>113</sub> | ou<br><sub>113</sub> | oy<br><sub>110</sub> | oi<br><sub>110</sub> |
| ee<br><sub>96</sub> | ss<br><sub>56</sub> | ll<br><sub>56</sub> | th<br><sub>117</sub> | qu<br><sub>97</sub> |

CPSIA information can be obtained
at www.ICGtesting.com
Printed in the USA
BVHW071922140920
588700BV00016B/787

9 781298 885326